IRELAND

THE TASTE &
THE COUNTRY

$\mathcal{I}$RELAND,

THE TASTE &
THE COUNTRY

MIKE BUNN

COLLINS & BROWN

To Betty – and to Ireland, for being herself.

First published in Great Britain in 1991 by
Anaya Publishers Ltd, 44-50 Osnaburgh Street
London NW1 3ND

This revised and updated edition published in 2000 by
Collins & Brown Ltd, London House, Great Eastern Wharf,
Parkgate Road, London SW11 4NQ
www.collins-and-brown.co.uk

Distributed in the United States and Canada by Sterling
Publishing Co, 387 Park Avenue South, New York 10016, USA

A CIP catalogue record of this book is available from the British
Library.

ISBN 1-85585-841-X

Art director Jane Forster
Directory Editor Hilary Sagar
Maps Sarah Willis

Typeset in Great Britain by Tradespools Ltd, Frome, Somerset
Colour reproduction by Columbia Offset, Singapore
Printed by Eurolitho, Italy

BERNARD KAVANAGH

BED & BREAKFAS

CAFÉ

CONTENTS

*W*HERE GRASSES GROW & WATERS FLOW IN A FREE & EASY WAY

*I*T'S HOME SWEET HOME WHERE'ER I ROAM THROUGH LANDS & WATERS WIDE

*A*ND BRIGHT IN THE SUN SHONE THE EMERALD PLAIN

FOREWORD

Wherever they may in the distance go, the world of this land is never forgotten by its born. And as Ireland emerges an oasis on the western tip of Europe and despite the ancient feud and one of the most astonishingly prolonged incompatibility of peoples this planet has ever known, the most of this scholarly saintly isle still is and remains compared to the rest of the globe, a relatively peaceful place. And as emerald green as it always was. No doubt there might be occasionally a deserved fist delivered in the gob, but for the most part decency and dignity are to be discovered everywhere. Indeed, if these two warring tribes had to choose their favourite people on this earth they would, a little shamefacedly, perhaps, choose each other.

Therefore we will forgive you your foregone conclusions. And wherever you are now don't listen to anyone telling you that this isn't the greatest place going yet to stay in or to get to for a complete pleasant change. To wake up to one of its pale cool dawns. The gulls squawking over the rooftops of its coastal towns and cities and the birds chirping across the countryside. And where the worst that can happen to you has often already happened before you've gone two inches and there is nothing further to worry about in any of the joyful undisturbed miles ahead. For inevitability is an Irishman's credo. And he'll tell you, you won't change fate by rushing into it. Best to wait, leisurely, for it to overtake you – preferably with your and his elbows propped on a bar.

Now having said that, I can say this. There is no doubt that the sun is shy in Irish skies. And the inclement often continual. But the nature of the weather can be the least of your concerns. And I'll tell you why. Ireland is a place where dreaming takes on a reality so real that it's all you'll ever need for entertainment. It would keep you indoors with a drink and in the company of other dreamers. And you'd be like your small Irish farmer. Standing nearby. In the middle of his making hay, it's rained. You'd see indifference written all over your man's face. And know that he's said to himself, well then that's that, let God have his way. And it's only for the sake of letting the neighbours know he is not to be trifled with, that your man when the first drops of rain fell, ran back and forth over fields shaking his fist against the sky and gesticulating his legs in his dance of rage.

But it's not only for the matter of a calm spirit, Ireland is grand for other reasons, too. Culture, ancient and modern, is all over the place. There are living and breathing examples of authors, painters, composers and poets, plus the odd sculptor lurking up the end of every main street and down many a country boreen. Each and every one of them in action, with instruments, poems and pictures at the ready to entertain you. Even the architects are in on the act. And some getting very exotic. New buildings good to look at are sneaking up here and there. Many of the old ones, even better to look at, are being cherished and have a citizenry and a Georgian Society fighting to keep them preserved and protected.

Now outwardly as things change, inwardly the Irishman remains the same. And in some ways this contradicting conundrum prepares you best for coming as a traveller to this isle. For what goes on here now seems to turn on its head nearly all that has preceded in the centuries. James Joyce, above all, has won his victory. He's now seen to be there in Dublin, standing life-sized in bronze surveying his city. This same man once accused of having the filthiest mind this century. But along with Joyce's words the Irish mind too has been unchained and is alive with a lustiness expressed in the very latest American vernacular. Poets are no longer rude but polite. They will for a modest fee read you their poems. Or a verse out of the literary past. Nor would he be churlish if you handed him one of your own sonnets to read. Except he might have to charge you a higher fee. So take it that this darling land has at last thrown off its ancient repressive coverings. And its grey veil of rain has drawn back to reveal a brand-new Ireland awake.

So, sitting pretty in its natural glory, the world can now come and take more than a peek at the most newly glamorous place in God's kingdom. And do so in a trice. Whirring helicopters and stiff-winged motor birds take off and land. Television signals criss-cross the sky and advertise the wonders of the outside world. But the natives, too, have originated their own brand of excellence of which to boast. And it is not only confined to great cheeses, crustaceans, beef, fish and lamb in which they triumph but also the soda bread, barmbrack and spice buns that melt in your mouth. Instead of your bumpy, lumpy damp mattresses sloping in the middle, hotels now provide magic slumbering where all earthly comfort is guaranteed. Plus now there is the softest of toilet tissue on tap, when once you'd find yourself crouching, mournful, in wind and rain, searching around, anxious, for a leaf of shrubbery to use.

But there is more. Even when left in his ignorance, the Irishman was always ahead of the whole world. And has held up his hand to object to the poisonous residues which grant nations their badges of progress. He has saved his cattle, horses and sheep to live for another and better day. He no longer lets the slates fall from the big houses that he did not burn. Nor with their roofs still on does he any longer send his cattle in to shelter and to manure on the parquet. Now he proudly installs himself. And beneath the Georgian glory of the plasterwork he may even knock back a glass or two of champagne. For every Irishman is a king. And lucky there is no empty throne available, for by God if there were, there would be a lethal stampede. Nor would there be any scarcity of Irish queens, either, in on the rush and getting in the way.

With the fair-minded nature of the populace, the Irish are, in general, a nice helpful bunch and they often don't mean to do the awful things they sometimes do. It is only that Ireland with its few mountains is a great place for making them out of its molehills. But now, as big things happen all over Europe, they wait patiently to take advantage of the best of them and as a small nation are doing more things right than you would dare believe. No need any longer to remind you of the fact that soda water and the electrical battery were first invented here. Or that here, too, took place the oft-mentioned first performance of Handel's *Messiah*. And although there are still heaps and loads of blarney and boasting to be heard coming around the corner of every snug of every pub, the Irish have at last achieved the heights in many and better walks of life, rearing up original as they always were. And under where glorious chandeliers still hang, instead of the forelock-pulling, they do be welcoming you to enjoy their carrots served like caviar. Or the leeks or lobster, which come finger-tip fresh from garden and sea.

And now you're wondering why would Ireland in the excellence of its food be any different than any other place. Well, for a start, it has some of the deepest, loamiest fertile soil in the world. And upon it does be falling gently year-round waters brought upon a moist mild wind from the Atlantic. And already nibbling upon this cornucopia, and leaping and bursting from cover, are your rabbits, pheasant, quail and snipe. And dying to be cooked. There be even Frenchmen and Germans who have come here and set about taking advantage of the great milk and cream to produce cheeses rivalling any on earth. And if you stood yourself in an Irish meadow you'd soon know why you were licking your chops at the sight of the chubby lambs and bullocks grazing. For, sniffing their way through the fields, they nurture themselves on grasses and herbs growing since Methuselah's time.

Now with the weather always suitable to do so, what would you be drinking. Well, there would be, if you know the right people, and that's nearly anybody, there would be poteen, the local firewater, to put you sooner than otherwise on your back. But best for your health would be to stay with stout, this dark beer which foams so creamily at the top of your glass. And now if you're wondering where would you especially go for these indubitable refreshments, for a start try Longueville House, Mallow or Rosleague Manor, Letterfrack, the country house hotels, homey and welcoming in their idyllic settings and wherein you dine by candlelight. Or for a fine pint of stout you could head to the pubs the Yukon or Canton Casey's in Mullingar. In the Yukon, as well as a library of best drink you can interest yourself in a library of American car licence plates. And in the metropolis of Dublin, there are still pubs with their traditions upheld. Try Ryan's of Parkgate Street, along the Liffey and just outside the gates of Phoenix Park. Here you'll find snugs. These are private, confessional little places for private people with private thoughts to express, and here in Ryan's they are especially reserved for nice deserving folk.

But if you're still footloose in Dublin, there remain other places of liquid invigoration not disembowelled for the sake of aggiornamento, as the Italians say. These are the sacred public houses of Mulligan's in Poolbeg Street, the Stag's Head off Dame Street and Doheny and Nesbitt's just down the road from the Shelbourne Hotel. Nor miss the oldest of them all, the Brazen Head up along the quays.

In Ireland you'd be making a great mistake to seriously overlook any of the pubs you pass by. Within is always another world not seen before and not to be experienced again. Even if empty the ghosts will whisper in your ear. If looking for the living, there be actors and actresses lurking about Neary's in Chatham Street. For prancing and preening models and film moguls, you have only to sit to a fine pint in the Bailey whose present day's existence is owed to the painter and writer John Ryan, the first Dublin publican ever to pay due homage to Ireland's great writers. And the fact there isn't some acknowledgement to this man up somewhere on this pub's wall is a great lack I hope soon to be corrected. But be sure of one thing, each public house attracts its own character of clientele, and if the people in it are wrong, the pub will be wrong too. So sniff first in the door. Of course, you'll be immediately invited in to put things right.

And now for a second let's rush back into the past. Once there was a great restaurant, Jammet's. The passing of which has brought many a tear to many a Dubliner's eye. But it has remained an inspiration to the many who have come afterwards. And who will now soon become equally revered. Locks restaurant on the canal. The Unicorn, an unpretentious and pleasant place habited by the natives. The Chinese, too, are here and their cuisine can be found up some stairs in Anne Street. But then if you're ready for elegance and luxury, the Shelbourne Hotel is where most of your needs and wants are met at once, and there be no need to stir a further inch. But if you do stir, out in the Meath countryside is Dunderry Lodge which will satisfy all you'd wish for and find in the best restaurants of France.

Guide you now across these landscapes, seascapes and moonscapes galore. And let you know that any season in this land has its joys. From the summertime flowerings of the honeysuckle and bursts of whitethorn in the hedgerows, to the sweet scent of turf glowing in a midwinter fire. And in a world that hurries and hurts where it hurts most, what nation anywhere deserves to pleasantly thrive better. Or merits that you come where the green gladness is and where the glooms shall enfold you not. Where the purple clover blossom sweetens the air at your feet and thistles tall as trees come raging out of the ground. Where under the sky can you find a land that will so kindly kiss your face.

Or be a place
That has got
To be forgiven
For its faults.

J. P. Donleavy

THE TASTE & THE COUNTRY

My obsession with Ireland developed from a fishing trip in May 1968, my first visit to the country. Like quicksilver dashed over rich green velour, the rivers and lakes of the midland plain presented themselves unpolluted, running crystal-clear and full of fish prepared to rise to the occasion. Lough Sheelin was my chosen spot – then the serious trout fisherman's mecca. Its fish were always in pristine condition, of polished chrome, with small heads and large brown spots, and their average weight considerably higher than anywhere else in Europe.

My boatman on that trip was Felix Harten, a small man of seventy-five years who had as many grandchildren. Two of his sons, Frank and Brian, were superb boatmen, though Felix was not. He did, however, make excellent tea! In Ireland, pulling up on to an island or any shoreline for lunch is part of the angling tradition and constitutes the main ritual of the day. A few dry sticks are gathered and a fire lit. With the smell of wood smoke sweetening the air, a blackened kettle is filled with lake water and placed on the now raging fire. When boiling, a handful or more of tea is thrown in to 'stew' – the brew is said never to be strong enough 'until you could trot a mouse on it'.

Felix would pick a sprig of gorse and shove it down the spout of the kettle to act as a strainer. He would often suggest, if the day was hot, that we should have black mint tea: far more refreshing. Wild water mint was readily available, growing everywhere along the shoreline. It is in fact very refreshing, but the crafty old fox didn't mention the fact that more often than not the milk had gone off.

During these pleasant interludes and in the bars late into the night I used to hear fascinating stories about wild men of hunting and shooting, of fishing and fishermen, of greyhounds and lurchers, of horse fairs and horses, of cockfights that went on for days – most of which were lies. On my return to London, I started to pine for this very special place that I knew so little about – I had to have more. And in due course, I did . . .